THE DYNAMICS OF
PRAYING IN
TONGUES

IBIYINKA ORELESI

The Dynamics of Praying in Tongues

By Ibiyinka Orelesi

© February 2024

Unless otherwise stated all scriptural references are taken from the Amplified version of the Bible.

© *ZOE COMMUNICATIONS*
waleorelesi@gmail.com

ACKNOWLEDGEMENTS

I wish to acknowledge the grace and strength that our Lord Jesus Christ through the Holy Spirit supplied to enable me put this work together for the benefit of mankind.

Thank You Jesus.

FOREWORD

Prayer is a sanctuary for vulnerable souls. It is the place where nothing is hidden. It is the point of crying out to God with words; and also, without words. It is the place of communicating with your sighs, your groans and your unsaid words. In His sovereignty; God understands the tears that fall from your eyes in the place of prayers.

Have you ever pondered the sheer potency of prayer? Imagine if every word, every utterance, was a spark, lighting up the spiritual realm, turning darkness into an illuminating spectacle.

The power we wield when we pray, especially when

we pray in tongues, is beyond human comprehension.

God has made provision for the highest form of communication there is, and that is praying in tongues. It equips you to pray about things in a way your understanding cannot. Praying in tongues enhances your sensitivity to God and keeps you on the same wavelength with the frequency of His Spirit. At the point of intense praying in tongues, your spirit locks with the Spirit of God and you have direct access into the deep things of God. The devil is confused at this point as you speak 'mysteries' unto God.

Have you ever found yourself in a foreign country where you need a tourist guide? Even though you are aware you can rely on your guide, your connection to that immediate environment is limited by your inability to speak the native language. To some degree, the language barrier restrains you from maximizing the fullness of the pleasure of your stay in that country. The bible says in **Romans 8:26**:
"... the Holy Spirit takes hold of us in our human frailty to empower us in our weakness. For example, at times we don't even know how to pray, or know the best things to ask for. But the Holy Spirit rises up within us ... pleading to God with

emotional sighs too deep for words." (The Passion Translation).

When the Holy Spirit prays through us as we speak in tongues, we are assured that He prays *'in perfect harmony with God's plan'*. Romans 8:27. As citizens of heaven, there is a native tongue that none other can comprehend. It is the language of the Spirit. It is a code that only God deciphers. When we pray in tongues, our messages become encrypted to the forces of darkness and our human understanding is deadened. Our spirits fully connect to God; Father to child, spirit to Spirit. That is the deepest level of communion.

In this book, light is shed on what it means to be a child of God, and how to walk in the fullness of that reality by shouting *Abba Father* through the spirit of adoption. As you read through the pages; it is my prayer that your eyes of understanding will be opened as you step into a higher dimension of walking in power. Remember the power of prayer is within your grasp. Seize this opportunity, and watch as your faith ascends to new heights.

Wale Orelesi
May 5, 2024

DEDICATION

To you O lord my Master

CONTENTS

In the
Beginning

1

IN THE BEGINNING

We hail from God. God is the author of creation. The bible contains numerous verses testifying to the truth that there is a loving God who existed before the world ever began, and whose mind conceived the idea of the creation of all there is in heaven and on earth.

Everything was carefully planned, to the last atom in the volume of details. In addition to this, every plan was meticulously implemented. All things were made by God and for Him. The New Living Translation of the bible did a fantastic rendition of Colossians 1:17. *"He existed before anything else, and he holds all creation together".*

God's mighty hands laid the foundation of the earth. Before the mountains were born, before ever there was a tiny drop of water in the oceans. God had always existed; all sufficient by Himself.

Everything that was made originated from God. John 1:3. Isaiah 49:14-16. Psalms 24:1. It is good to understand that aside being the author of creation, recounting the account of creation; the bible laid bare another truth, and that is the fact that everything created through the hands of God was preconceived. Nothing occurred by accident. Like an expert artist, God wove the tapestry with careful details. Like an intentional potter, He moulded every vessel from clay and determine their worth and function. The intricacies of His creation are beyond what the human mind can ever fully grasp.

"In the beginning God (prepared, formed, fashioned, and) created the heavens and the earth". Genesis 1:1.

God spoke creation into existence. Everything He made was called forth. However, when it was time to create man, God reached deep into the core of His being and brought forth man from His very identity. That is what the bible means by saying *'God created*

12

man in His own image'.

26 "God said, let Us [Father, Son and Holy Spirit] make mankind in Our image, after Our likeness...
27 God created man in His own image, in the image and likeness of God created He him; male and female created He them..." Genesis 1:26-27.

Before you proceed, do kindly note that within the context of this book; 'man' refers to humans in the generic form. To be created in the image and likeness of God means to be made in His similitude, after the form of His Spirit. Man is a spirit because he was born of the Spirit of God. Man originated from the Spirit of the Almighty.

During the creation of man, God reached into His core and produced a being fashioned after the very essence of His Spirit. He did not stop at that level, He breathed upon man and as an entity conceived and brought into existence by God, man from that point became a living soul. The created human is of a tripartite nature. He has a spirit, lives in a body and possesses a soul.

Man is a spirit, He lives in a body and he processes a soul. The spirit of man is the unseen part of him that is as real as the part that can be seen and felt. It is actually the 'real' being. In addition to that, it is a part of him that will live forever. It will be in existence even after the physical death of the human body. The eternal human spirit is the identifier before God while the temporary physical body of man is the identifier before his fellow humans. The body of man (made of dust) is required of him in order to be able to live on this terrestrial plane. On the other hand, the soul of man (which is the seat of the intellect and emotions) is of three parts consisting of the mind, the will and the emotions. Proverbs 24:14.

The human spirit is the never-dying part of man that was brought forth from the Spirit [Greek: *ruach*] of God. Man is also a spirit being and the earthly body he exists in is just the outer case that houses the spirit. The bible also refers to the human body as 'the earthly tent'. 2 Corinthians 5:1. The earthly body consists of the sense organs. This 'tent' (or tabernacle) that houses the real thing; that is, the human spirit decays after man's earthly sojourn. Because it was made of dust, upon death it will return to dust. The spirit however will return unto his Maker when the earthly days of man's pilgrimage are fulfilled.

God as the source of the human spirit

When Adam and Eve fell in the garden, their spirits were cut off from the life (Greek: *Zoe*) that flows from God. Man needs his spirit to be alive and remain in tune with God in order to connect with Him on a deeper (meaningful) level. After the fall in the Garden of Eden, man died. That death is not physical but spiritual. Anyone who comes back to God through the acceptance of salvation will have his/her spirit quickened (made alive) and restored into fellowship with God. At the point of becoming born again, the *Zoe (life)* of God is restored to the sinner who was previously cut off from the flow but has now received God's offer of salvation. This is the mystery of the new birth in a nutshell.

The transaction that took place in the garden

The source of a thing is the sustenance thereof. Man was never created to exist in isolation or find peace outside God. Man was created for fellowship, for a meaning drawn from a Source that is higher than him. It was never God's intention for the man He created to be all-sufficient. We were never created to thrive outside of God. It was never designed for humans to find peace, joy and fulfilment in anyone or anything outside God who is the ultimate source of our lives. Of a truth, *'in Him we live and have our being ...'* Acts 17:28. Our very existence hinges on the totality of God's being.

There is a vacuum inside humans which no one and no other thing except God alone can fill. There is a yearning for connection with the divine which nobody except God can satisfy. This explains why everyone longs for a spiritual relationship that is personal, fulfilling and enduring. After the need to be unconditionally loved and accepted, having the feeling of belonging to a community or a family of some sort, the next need crucial to everyone is the need to be accepted and understood.

In the Garden of Eden, we are told that God steps down in the cool of the day. The garden He has made was for His creatures to dwell in. When God stepped in after they have taken the forbidden fruit, Adam and Eve became afraid and tried to hide. Though God could see their act of disobedience to Him, He still reached out to them. He called to Adam and Eve and asked *'where are you'*? Rather than rejoice at the voice of God and come out with ecstasy to fellowship, they responded by saying they heard God's voice but were afraid. In a bid to cover for the sin of rebellion against God, rather than run into the loving arms of God, both Adam and Eve fled. Genesis 3:6-10.

Psalms 139:7-12 sums up the folly of anyone trying to outwit God and conceal his or her sins. None can ever hide from the presence of God. He dwells everywhere, His eyes see everything, and even darkness is light unto His all-seeing eyes. Darkness hides nothing from Him and the night shines as the day. Of a truth *'the darkness and the light are both alike to God'*.

When the devil came into the garden to deceive Adam and Eve, he twisted the words God spoke to them earlier concerning the trees of the garden. Rather than believe all of God's words, Eve reasoned out there must be another life that is more fulfilling and unrestrained which they could explore and enjoy. At the moment of consenting to the devil's suggestions, that very moment when she ate the fruit, they were cut off from the presence of the Lord and the entire human race was sold out to sin.

When sin entered, the *Zoe* (life) that Adam and Eve carried was cut off from the source and their spirits were disconnected from the life-giving Spirit of God. Because God is holy and cannot behold iniquity, they were separated from His life, the cord that connects humanity to divinity from which flows life from the Spirit of God into their spirits. Their very essence was uprooted and truly, in the spirit realm they became dead and naked. They were stripped from the glory of God that shielded their nakedness. Having being stripped of the life and glory of God, humanity was sold into the slavery of sin.

And what is sin?

1 John 3:4 defines sin as *'the transgression of the law'*. In order to understand what the transgression of God's holy laws refers to, a quick look at The Message Translation of the same bible passage will suffice. It explains verse succinctly. It says *'all who indulge in a sinful life are dangerously lawless, for sin is a major disruption of God's order'*. Adam and Eve went against God's order for their existence. They took God out of the picture and chose another lord. By accepting the offer of sin, they transferred ownership to the devil. They transitioned from being God-owned to being ruled by the god of this world. They chose another kingdom from which their existence never originated.

"Everyone who commits (practices) sin is guilty of lawlessness; for [that is what] sin is, lawlessness

(the breaking, violating of God's law by transgression or neglect – being unrestrained and unregulated by His commands and His will)".

Anyone who has been cut off from the life of God is 'dead'. That person's spirit is not alive and can never connect to the source. Sin is not about the fruits. It goes beyond committing fornication or worshipping other idols (plus many other works of iniquity). Those are the manifestation of the works of the flesh. Sin is being in enmity with God. Anyone who has been cut off from the *ruach* of God has become an outcast [an alien] to the citizenship of heaven. It is not what you do that makes you a sinner; you are a sinner because you sin. It is the unregenerated Adamic nature in you that cuts you off from God. A sinner is the person who has been driven away from God's presence.

The propitiation for man's sins

The greatest joy heaven has is a sinner who finds his way back home! In Luke chapter 15, the bible tells stories of things that got missing and were later found. We read an account of a shepherd who has a hundred sheep and lost one. He left the ninety nine and went in search of the one that went astray. The woman who has ten coins but lost one swept everywhere and got a lamp to search for the one that got missing. In the same way, the father of the prodigal son was excited to see his stray son walking back into his loving arms. We are told that in the same way, *'there is joy in heaven when one sinner repents'*. Luke 15:8.

The eyes of God are too pure to behold iniquity. When man fell into sin and was cut off from the life of God, God gave His precious begotten Son as the propitiation for our sins. What that means is that Jesus gets to die in our stead and took upon Himself our sins in order to reconcile us back to God. He is the Lamb of God which took away the sin of the world. John 1:29, 36. As the sacrificial lamb, His blood made atonement for our sins and paid the full wages of sin which is death.

God took it upon Himself to bring us back to Himself in an intimate, vibrant fellowship so that we can be restored to Him in fellowship the way it was before the fall in the garden. For the transaction that took place in the Garden of Eden, another one took place on the cross when the Son of God gave His blood as the full atonement (payment) for the sin of the world. It wasn't the fruits of sin that were dealt with. No. at

the cross, the root of sin was addressed. Jesus went into hell and took over what was given to the devil. He faced God's wrath on the cross and became the sin of the world; from the first man that ever lived, to the last man that will ever live. His blood paid for their sin in full!
Alleluia!

Salvation and the acceptance of God's love

In the same way that man willingly took over the nature of sin, it is expedient for him to also freely receive the gift of salvation. Salvation is a gift. It must be received. It cannot be forced on people. Being saved is by grace and it is received through faith. In addition, salvation is the gift of God. It does not come by any work that you have done to merit being forgiven and received back into the family of God. Ephesians 2:8-9. When you get born again, like the sheep that was lost, you return back home to your Shepherd and the One who paid a great price for your soul. Anyone who received the gift of salvation has retraced his steps and 'came back home'.

"For you were going astray like sheep ... but now you have come back to the Shepherd and Guardian ... of your soul". 1 Peter 2:25.

What happens at the new birth?

Becoming integrated in fellowship with God is not as cumbersome as many think. It is a smooth transition that has been fully paid for. It involves a conscious acceptance of God's offer of salvation through His Son Jesus. In the book of John chapter 3, Nicodemus came to Jesus at night asking questions on how to become born again. His spirit longed to be connected to God's Spirit but he did not understand how. It was a simple question. *'How can a man be born when he is old? Can he enter the second time into his mother's womb, and be born?'* John 3:4.

Becoming a child of God

There are fundamental questions you need to find answers to so that you can know how vital your salvation is to God. The first of such is your worthiness to be saved. Do not buy the lies of the devil. The bible made us to understand that Jesus was the Lamb slain before the foundation of the world. Revelation 13:8.

God knew about the fall before Adam and Eve ate the forbidden fruit. In addition to that, He made provision for your sins. The blood of Jesus is enough. It is enough to wipe your sins and make you acceptable unto God. Because God saw that you are worthy of being saved through His grace, He made provision for your salvation. Therefore, understand the first point that you are worthy.

Furthermore, it is not in the character of God that any sinner should go to hell. As long as they receive the provision He has made for the remission of their sins, they are welcomed into the fold. Like the shepherd that left ninety nine sheep to look for the lost one, God is always searching for you. He is always reaching out to you. He is eager to have you restored in fellowship so that the fullness of His Spirit can find expression you. He wants everyone to be saved and come to the knowledge of the truth. 1 Timothy 2:4.

'Everyone' includes you. It is irrespective of race, class or sex. The love of Jesus is all-encompassing. God wants to reach out to you at the core of your being. He wants to talk to you. In the same way, He longs to hear your voice. He wants a living, active relationship with you; in the same way that a loving father will reach out to the child he loves tenderly. Sincerely, God wants all men to come to the knowledge of truth. 1 John 3:4-5.

4 "Everyone who commits sins is guilty of

lawlessness for ... sin is lawlessness (the breaking, violating of God's law ...)
5... He appeared in visible form and became Man to take away [upon Himself] sins ... " 1 John 3:4-5.

Jesus came to take away sins; yours inclusive. Realizing the authenticity of this claim, Saul (who later became Paul) embraced the truth of salvation by stating *'... Christ Jesus came into the world to give salvation to sinners, of whom I am the chief'.* (Bible in Basic English.)

We are assured that God will richly forgive. It means He will abundantly pardon us even if our sins are like scarlet, they shall become white as snow. If they are red as crimson, they shall be like wool. Isaiah 1:18.

It is quite easy to receive God's salvation. You only need to believe with your heart unto righteousness, and with the mouth make confession unto salvation. Romans 10:10. The moment this is done and you open up your heart unto God, you become engrafted into God. Your spirit man comes alive and you become a partaker of God's nature, the way it was designed in the beginning, and your spirit and God's Spirit are fused to become one; forever inseparable.

A Deeper Understanding of Prayer

2

A Deeper Understanding of Prayer

IN MANY FORMS, humans have longed to 'touch' God in every way they could. There is a desire to call upon Him in the good times and be assured of His presence. There is also a longing to beckon on Him in times of trouble and be assured that He is near, and willing to save. Whether in good or bad times, there is a yearning for God in every human.

We love to call on God in an intimate way because we understand there is an assurance of being heard and understood. Prayer is a state of being vulnerable to lay all concerns bare. It is the moment of revealing our deepest thoughts to a Higher Being who can render assistance. It is the pouring out of our souls.

In Shiloh, because Hannah was in agony, she wept sore and prayed unto God. While rendering prayers, Hannah spoke in her heart, only her lips moved. Her voice was not audible. When mistaken for a drunk, she replied Eli the prophet '... I am a woman of a sorrowful spirit ... I have poured out my soul before the Lord.' 1 Samuel 1:15. She asked God to remove her shame as a woman who has been taunted by her rival for being unable to bear a child. God did not give her one or two children. Her expectation was surpassed. In addition to Samuel, she had other children.

The bible testifies that all flesh will come to God because He answers prayers. Psalms 65:2. Hearing our voices gladdens His heart and He responds when we call on Him in absolute trust. In addition to longing to have audience with us; we are assured that if we ask anything in line with His eternal counsel, He will answer us. 1 John 5:1.

Not only is God going to answer us, He will answer us with 'terrible deeds in righteousness'. Psalms 65:5. He will go over and above to grant our heart's requests. When we call upon the name of God, He answers with 'fearful and glorious' things. When we take the initiative to engage His presence and seek His face in the place of prayer, He honours our faith by answering us with dreadful deeds executed through His awesome power. You can count on Him to turn His ears when you beckon on Him.

Through the pages of the bible, we see several other

people (like Hannah) who called upon God in the time of anguish. We saw many who went through perilous time and came out unscathed. The children of Israel went through the Red Sea as if they travelled on dry ground. Up to this present generation, it is a miracle that blows our mind every time we read that account. The story of Daniel's mighty deliverance shows God as a prayer-answering God. Prior to being thrown inside the den, the bible records that Daniel was a man totally given to unceasing prayers. It was no surprise that when he was thrown into the lions' den, he came out unhurt.

During the heat of the battle in Joshua 10:11-14, Joshua commanded the sun and the moon to stand still and they obeyed his voice. In the same way that Hannah owes the birth of Samuel to prayer. Jabez's life received a transformation because he called on God to positively change the course of his life. Throughout history, and up to the present age, men and women have been in the business of calling on God. Everyone who came to Him with a perfect heart and according to the guidelines of prayer outlined in the bible had their voices heard on high; in addition, they had their requests extravagantly granted.

Do you desire to see God move on your behalf? Do you

wish you could enforce victory over every aspect of your life? Do you want a transformation regarding your affairs? Would you like to 'touch' God? When the woman with the issue of blood drew out virtue from Him, Jesus turned around and asked 'who touched Me'? Luke 8:45. Unlike other people thronging Him, Jesus knew when someone came and pulled substance out of Him. He was aware someone in that crowd did more than touch the fringes of the garments; she latched on to the supernatural and tapped from the source of life.

In the seventeenth chapter of the book of Acts, there is an account of the people of Athens who have different objects of worship. There were all over the place. In the best way known to them, they were trying to connect with God and feel His heartbeat. Their souls desperately craved God. The humanity in them hungered and wanted to touch divinity. They were so eager to feel the 'pulse' of God so much so that on a particular altar, they wrote an inscription to 'an unknown God'. In a bid to enlighten them about their ignorance and also throw light on the fact that God is truly alive and closer to them than the breath in their nostrils; Paul clears the air and states:

27 "... that they should seek God, in the hope that

they might feel after Him and find Him, although He is not far from each one of us.

28 For in him we live and move and have our being..." Acts 17:27-28.

God is close to us. He is the very air we breathe!

The Almighty God is not like an image made from gold, silver, or stone; or any image that is the product of human imagination and skills. Of a truth, we live, move and exist because of Him. In simple terms, 'we are because He is'. As a loving Father, He longs to hear us call His name. He wants us to open our arms wide as we run to Him and cry out 'Abba Father'. God longs for our presence. He wants to have intimate conversation with us. That is a rare privilege. In the same way that we long for God, He equally sends an open invitation to us. *"Call to Me and I will answer you, and tell you [and even show you] great and might things, [things which have been confined and hidden], which you do not know and understand and cannot distinguish."* Jer. 33:3.

How can we enjoy a thriving intimacy with God?

Basically, there are two major ways to grow in God. The first way you can connect with Him and feel His heartbeat is through hearing His voice. His voice resonates through the pages of the bible. Reading God's word enables you to understand His ways and align with His ordinances. His words contain instructions, precepts and guidelines that will flood your path with light. The second way of connecting in deep fellowship with God is via talking to Him.

Communicating with God is a two—way road. God wants you to hear Him talk to you, as much as He longs to hear your voice by speaking to Him. The ability to hear from God and also speak to Him makes all the difference as the consistent engagement in both will unleash a new vitality in your growth as a child of God.

The words of God are spirit and they are life. Through them, we are equipped with divine promises relating to every aspect of our lives. Through them also, we are equipped with the weapons of warfare. Christians receive inspiration and revelation from the scriptures and are strengthened in their walk with God.

God's words are potent. The Amplified version of the Holy Bible testifies that every word that God speaks 'is alive and full of power'. In other words, those words are 'active, operative, energizing and effective'. They are agile and infused with the spirit of God. The words of God are laden with life-giving power and can 'penetrate to the dividing line of the breath of life [soul] and the [immortal spirit]'. It does not stop at that level. God's words have the capacity to sift and analyze and judge the very thoughts and purposes of our hearts. Hebrews 4:12.

The bedrock of our relationship with God is having an unhindered flow of communication with our Maker. That entails hearing God speak to us as much as we also speak to Him.

Understanding prayer

Praying to God is powerful. It gives humans the unhindered access to appear before the throne of grace and talk to the Maker of the heavens and the earth. As an extension of communing with Him, God speaks back to man instructing, comforting and equipping him with the information required for thriving at every point in time.

Prayer provides the atmosphere of baring your soul and expressing your deepest feelings to the One who can see your unsaid thoughts before you weave the words together to consult Him in the place of prayer.

Nothing you say in the place of prayer is mundane. God can connect with the details of every tear that drop while conversing with Him.

How can someone who loves God connect with Him in prayer at the deepest level there ever is? That exactly is the core of this amazing book. Studying the act of prayer through the bible, one comes to the realization that there are numerous types of prayers. Beyond individual prayer, there is corporate prayer. There is also intercessory prayer in addition to prayer of supplication amongst others. However, within the context of this book; a close attention will be paid to individual prayer (specifically, praying in tongues).

Having established that prayer is made to God, how can we have uninhibited access to God at every point in time? Armed with the fact that God wants to have us come to Him in the place of prayer, there is need to enumerate the dynamics of prayer and how to tap into each of these.

First of all, we need to understand that prayer is made to God through the name of Jesus. That name is the only name through which anyone can be saved. It is also the only name endorsed by God through which we can approach Him in prayer. It has been appointed that 'at the name of Jesus every knee should bow...things in heaven and things on earth ...every tongue should confess Jesus is Lord'. Phil.2:10-11. (Paraphrased).

In several bible passages, we are directed to make our requests known to God in the place of prayer by using the name of Jesus. We are assured that whatever we request for in the name of Jesus will be granted. Not only that, having received our request; we are further comforted by the assurance that follows getting answered prayers. The bible made us understand that when we receive all that we have prayed for, our joy will be FULL.

23 "... you can go directly to the Father and ask him...he will give you what you ask for because you use my name.
24 ... Ask, using my name, and you will receive, and your cup of joy will overflow." John 14:23-24. (TLB)

Every time we approach the throne of God with prayer requests that align with His plan and purpose for our lives, we have an assurance that heaven is at attention. The audacity to come boldly to God is borne out of the invitation He has already extended to us. We can come based on the assurance that we will not be turned back. Without inhibition, we can approach God concerning anything as long as they align with His will. We know and we are sure that He will grant our heart's desire and honour His promise in our lives.

14 "And this is the confidence (the assurance, the privilege of boldness) which we have in Him: [we are sure] that if we ask anything (make any request) according to His will (in agreement with his own plan), He listens to and hears us.
15 And if (since) we [positively] know that He listens to us in whatever we ask, we also know [with settled and absolute knowledge] that we have [granted us as our present possessions] the requests made of Him." 1 John 5:14-15.

In addition to praying with the name of Jesus, we need to pray to God with His promises when we pray. We must send His words back to Him. When we call on God, we appropriate His promises and pray them over our lives. In this context, prayer is actual warfare. We need to pray from the point of triumph and enforce the victory of the cross spanning every area of our lives.

Another potent weapon regarding prayer is to

actually pray in the spirit and pray in tongues as well. Though they appear similar, both differ. However, both entail having a crystal understanding of the person and the operations of the Holy Spirit.

Who is the Holy Spirit?

Understanding the person of the Holy Spirit is crucial in order to draw virtues from Him. He is God Himself; the third person in the trinity and the engineering force in the Godhead. He is actually one and the same with God the Father and Jesus; God the Son. He is co-equal with God the father and also God the Son. Although He is referred to by many names in God's words, He remains as One entity. In Genesis 1:2 and 1 Samuel 10:10, He is called the *'Spirit of God'*. Isaiah 61:1 calls Him the *'Spirit of the Lord'*. He is called the *'Holy Spirit'* in Psalms 51:11 and Mathew 28:19. Philippians 1:19 calls Him the *'Spirit of Jesus Christ'*.

Just as much in essence and person as God the Father and God the Son, Mathew 28:19-20 tells the disciples to *'go therefore and make disciples of all nations, baptizing them in the name of God the Father and of the Son and of the Holy Spirit...'* The Holy Spirit is God and as God, He is all powerful (Luke 1:35-37). In addition to that, He is holy (Romans 1:4).

Furthermore, the Holy Spirit is eternal (Hebrews 9:14) and He knows all things (1 Corinthians 2:10-11).

The Holy Spirit was with God during creation. Also, in the days of His earthly existence, He was with Jesus when He came in the flesh as God with us. After Christ's ascension, the Holy Spirit is given to abide with us and He is God within us. God is no longer far from us, He resides in us. He is our constant companion, our friend and comforter.

The word of God sheds more light to the person of the Holy Spirit. He is the Counselor, the Spirit of truth who lives in us. John 14:16-17. When the Holy Spirit comes into the heart of a believer, that person is engulfed with the totality of God. God's Spirit activates the force of heaven in a believer's life. The in-dwelling of God the Father and God the Son is made evident through the workings of the Holy Spirit.

Before going back to heaven, Jesus assured the believers that He will send the Holy Spirit who will abide with them and teach them everything about the God-head. The Holy Spirit is a Helper, Advocate, Strengthener and Standby. He holds our hands and helps us in the Christian race. He reveals God to us. He reveals the scriptures to us and He energizes us in our inner man. He supplies the strength we need for our spiritual growth. In a nutshell, the Holy Spirit is God Himself. This knowledge is a mystery.

After His resurrection, Jesus showed Himself to the disciples with unquestionable evidences and infallible proofs. For forty days, He appeared to them and told them many things about the kingdom of God. Prior to that time, He had spoken to them about the Holy Spirit. Prior to his ascension, He commanded the disciples not to leave Jerusalem but rather to wait and receive the *'promise of the Father'*. Acts 1:4.

The Holy Spirit is the promise of the Father unto believers. Assuring the disciples of how the in-filling of the Spirit will happen, Jesus states: *'for John truly baptized with but you shall be baptized with the Holy Spirit'.* Acts 1:4. Indicating what the Holy Spirit will do, Jesus assures the believers that when the Holy Spirit fills them up, they will be endued with power and equipped to witness to other unbelievers who are scattered all over the world. In other words, the Holy Spirit enables every child of God to become a partner in witnessing to other people about the saving power of Jesus. The Spirit of God; the promise of the Father equips us as Christians for global evangelism. Acts 1:4-5.

After adhering to the instructions of Jesus, when the day of Pentecost was fully come, all the disciples were together in one place. All of a sudden, there was a mighty sound like the blowing of a violent wind which came from heaven. It filled the place they were gathered and all of them saw what seemed to be tongues of fire that separated and came to rest on each of them. At that instant, every single soul in that gathering was filled with the Holy Spirit and they began to speak in other tongues. That was the beginning of a higher realm of relating with God.

At the point of being filled up, God came inside every believer to reside therein. That was the entry point of an endless experience of the supernatural. The feeling of being filled with the Holy Spirit is beyond words. Getting filled with the Spirit of the living God with the vocal evidence of speaking in tongues takes Christianity to a whole new level. Acts 2:1-4.

Understanding the function of the Holy Spirit

The Holy Spirit is the in-filling of God. He is exactly God in us. 1 Corinthians 6:19. In addition, as previously established, He is the engineering force in the Godhead. Genesis 1:1. One of His major functions is to lead us into all truth (John 16:13-15). In addition to bringing things to our remembrance, (John 14:26), He points sinners to the Saviour and leads them to repentance (Romans 13:12) after convicting them of sin. (John 16:8-11).

What does it mean to pray in the Spirit?

Praying to God receives a dynamic force when it is fuelled by the promptings, inspiration and the strength of the Holy Spirit. Prayer is engulfed with a supernatural force that cannot be denied when it is birthed through God's Spirit. What then does it mean to pray in the Spirit?

Praying in the Spirit does not imply something grandeur reserved only for the saints of old, or a few chosen people. It is a privilege to be enjoyed by all the children of God. The bible says *'as many as are led by the Spirit of God, they are the sons of God'.* Romans 8:14.

To pray in the Spirit means to pray according to the will of God concerning a situation per season. It means praying the heart of God in (and for) every situation as prompted by the Holy Spirit who lives in us and knows what our limited human heart cannot fathom concerning a situation.

Praying in the Spirit can be done by praying in understanding. It can also be done by praying in tongues. Having explained what it means to pray in the Spirit, what then does it mean for someone to pray in understanding?

To pray in understanding means to pray in an earthly language that one is versed in and perfectly understands. However, praying in tongues means, praying to God concerning a situation (or communicating with Him) while speaking in an unknown tongues [the language of the Holy Spirit].

In order to shed light on these gray areas of praying in tongues, praying in the Spirit and praying in understanding; the bible passage below does an amazing analysis of 1 Corinthians 14:14-15 for easy comprehension.

14 "... if I pray in an [unknown] tongue, my spirit [by the Holy Spirit within me] prays, but my mind is unproductive...
15 ... I will pray with the spirit [by the Holy Spirit that is within me], but I will also pray [intelligently] with my mind and understanding..."

The Benefits of Praying in Tongues

3

The Benefits of Praying in Tongues

HAVING LAID THE foundation of a deeper understanding of prayer in the previous chapter, it is clearly understood that prayer connects us to God in an organic manner. Whether we pray in understanding or pray in tongues, the most important thing for us as children of God is to pray in the Spirit; that is, according to the leading of the Holy Spirit in line with God's counsel for a particular person or issue per time.

Also, having established that we are expected to pray in the Spirit, there is another fool-proof way of upgrading the status of our prayers. It is expressly achieved by understanding how to pray in tongues, and how to consciously tap into this powerhouse.

Many Christians have been wrongly taught that speaking (and praying) in tongues is reserved for veterans in the faith. This is absolutely wrong. Every child of God has access to God and should pray in tongues.

Why every Christian should speak in tongues

The vocal evidence of speaking in tongues is the physical proof of the infilling and baptism of the Holy Spirit. This is seen in the book of Acts 2:4. As a form of partaking in this promise of the Father unto all who believes (Mark 16:17), speaking in tongues should gladden the heart of every child of God. It is 'mysteries' directed unto God. Like a direct encrypted line of a telephone, it gives unhindered access when communication is taking place between God and His child. Taking great joy in this treasure, Paul writes *'I thank my God, I speak with tongues more than ye all'.* 1 Corinthians 15:18.

Praying in the tongues infuses supernatural force into your prayers in addition to establishing the growth of your Christian faith. After receiving the gift of salvation, the next phase is receiving the gift of the Holy Spirit. This can be received by waiting on God in the place of prayer. It can also come through the laying on of the hands of men of God. Many people have simply received the Holy Spirit in the place of meditating on the scriptures. No strict rules apply in this matter. If your heart longs for this gift, God's abundant mercy will fulfill your desire. Being filled with the Holy Spirit is a good thing and God longs to have you filled and overflow in it. [Chapter 4 will elaborate on this].

"If you then, evil as you are, know how to give good gifts [gifts that are to their advantage] to your children, how much more will your heavenly Father give the Holy Spirit to those who ask and continue to ask Him!" Luke 11:13.

God wants all of us to receive the gift of the Holy Spirit, and in addition to that; He wants us to speak with new tongues. On the day of Pentecost, when all the believers who gathered were filled with the Holy Spirit, the bible records that there appeared unto them cloven tongues like as of fire and it sat upon each of them. After being filled with the Holy Spirit, this is what happened:
"And they were all filled with the Holy Ghost, and began to speak with other tongues, as the Spirit gave them utterance." Acts 2:4.

After many souls were worn to the Lord in Samaria through the ministry of Philip, in order to strengthen the souls that were saved, Peter and John were sent by the apostles to lay hands on the new converts in order for them to receive the gift of the Holy Spirit.

14 "Now when the apostles which were at Jerusalem heard that Samaria had received the word of God, they sent unto them Peter and John. 17 Then laid they their hands on them, and they received the Holy Ghost." Acts 8:14,17.

The gift of the Holy Spirit is freely given by God. It cannot be bought. In Samaria, Simon was eager to make a commercial venture out of the Holy Spirit. When he saw that people received the gift of the Holy Spirit through the laying on of hands, he offered the apostles money and asks them to also give him the ability to impart people with the Holy Spirit by laying hands on them. His request received a sharp rebuke from Peter because his heart is not right with God.

"But Peter said to him, 'may your money be destroyed along with you, because you thought you could buy the [free] gift of God with money!" Acts 8:20.

The innumerable benefits of praying in tongues

The Holy Spirit takes your hands in the place of prayer and enables you to pray in alignment with God's thought at every point in time. 'God is a Spirit'. This foundational statement has been reiterated times and again in the earlier chapters of this book.

Whenever a born again child of God prays in tongues, the regenerated spirit in that person connects directly with the Spirit of God. It thus becomes a case of 'deep calling unto the deep'. Every time you pray in tongues, your spirit is praying to your Source (God). From the core of your being, you are speaking forth out of your spirit 'mysteries' unto God. You speak forth those mysteries as the Holy Spirit gives you 'utterance'.

Praying in tongues elevates the act of prayer in many ways. There are scores of reasons why you need to stretch your spiritual muscles and love this 'exercise'. Praying in this manner must be intentional and consistent. Engaging in this spiritual exercise is rewarding for a host of reasons:

-        **Direct access to God**

Praying in tongues connects your spirit directly to the Spirit of God. It fuses your heart to the heart of God in a way that can only be made possible when kindred spirits connect. In the place of prayer, when you switch on to praying in tongues, you hit the target. You can never pray amiss by praying in tongues. It allows you to speak directly to God; in a father to child manner.

"... One who speaks in an unknown tongue does not speak to people but to God; for no one understands him or catches his meaning, but by the Spirit he speaks mysteries [secret truths, hidden things]."
1 Cor. 14:2.

The bible says we have received the spirit of adoption and we can cry out unto God; Abba Father. Romans 8:15.

In the Aramaic language, the word that shows intimate relationship between a father and child is 'Abba'. It connotes deep intimacy. It is just like a child running towards a loving father and shouting in ecstasy 'daddy'! In examining the process and the benefits of this glorious state, one marvels at how The Passion Translation captures Romans 8:15.

"... you have received the 'Spirit of full acceptance', enfolding you into the family of God ... our spirits join him in saying the words of tender affection, 'Beloved Father!'"

To this end, because we are children of God and heirs of God; we can run to God in the deepest form of intimacy there is in the place of prayer and pour our hearts out without fear of any inhibition.

- **Speaking mysteries unto God**

Through the Holy Spirit, we have not only been given access to God, we can now speak 'mysteries' unto our Father. It is impossible to be in the know of events that are yet to unfold. However, because the Holy Spirit lives in us and knows everything, He nudges our hearts and prompts us on what we need to pray about. Not only that, the Holy Spirit goes further to pray through us by speaking 'mysteries', the hidden truths about the situation or thing we are praying for unto God. When we yield our tongues unto Him, He takes over and prays accurately regarding that manner.

We can deposit prayers into the future about things that are currently sketchy. Take for instance; if you are unsure of what career direction to focus on, you can pray about it to God. You can ask for His leading and ask Him to help you make the right decisions that will lead you into a profitable career later on. In the same vein, you can commit a journey into the hands of God and ask Him to make all the details work in your favour.

A pregnant woman can start investing prayer over her unborn child by laying her hands on the baby in the womb and speak mysteries unto God regarding that unborn child. Your prayer will be effective to position everything that heaven ordained for the child to align in due course after being born. When it comes to praying about things you cannot provide details about or fully comprehend, you can yield your tongue to God and let the Holy Spirit pray through you.

2 "If you praise him in the private language of tongues, God understands you but no one else does, for you are sharing intimacies just between you and him." 1 Corinthians 14:2.

- **Praying in tongue strengthens your spirit**

"But ye, beloved, building up yourselves on your most holy faith, praying in the Holy Ghost."
Jude 1:20.

Praying in tongues edifies you. When you start praying, you will discover that you start from a lower level of utterance. As you progress, there is going to be a progression and your spirit continually progress, rise like an edifice higher and higher. As you stay connected to God in the place of prayer, your spiritual batteries are charged. As you become more attuned, you gain the ability to pick signals and align with the spiritual frequency of the spirit, where enigmatic truths are revealed.

Praying in tongues could be likened to a form of spiritual exercise where you engage your spiritual muscles and get them fit for usage. When you pray in tongues, your muscles are active and healthy for use.

Praying in tongues keep you spiritually alert and sensitive to hear what God is trying to pass across to you. It helps you not to be dull of hearing, blind to seeing and oblivious of spiritual activities. Praying in tongues gets your spiritual antenna on to pick signals at a higher frequency that a natural human cannot operate in.

At its root, in the Greek language, *oikodomeo* is the word that means 'edify'. As a compound word consisting two separate words *'oikos'* [house] and *'domeo'* [to build], the meaning reflects clearly. *Oikodomeo* refers to building a house (or a gigantic edifice). Usually, building is done with stone laid upon stone and precept laid upon precept. It is a process where something is layered on top of another to create something solid and magnificent.

In a broader sense, *oikodomeo* means 'to edify', 'to establish' 'to make well-grounded'. These are the things praying in tongues does for a believer. It keeps the person grounded in the truth of God's reality, established and fortified to last while creating value.

Praying in tongues ensures that you are constantly **'switched on' 'strong' and 'grounded'**. Praying in tongues builds you as a child of God. It brings together everything needed to infuse stability into your spirit man and keep your life stable.

-        **You will not pray amiss**

When you do not know exactly what to pray for, the Holy Spirit runs along swiftly and guides you. Because you are speaking deep utterances that are accurate and rightly addresses the situation, praying in tongues hastens the answers to your prayers. It gets you exactly the perfect answer for the situation you are prayer on. Praying in tongues helps you to be in the know of events that are yet to unfold and furthermore help you to properly address those issues. Not only will the Holy Spirit give you a nudge, He will pray through you. Through the help of this amazing third Person of the trinity, encrypted messages are decoded. Issues that should be hazy and keep you confused receive the light of God and get sorted.

I remember the story of a dear young lady who while praying received a nudge to pray for her future marriage. She hearkened and started praying. After the prayer, God told her a friend will come by in that evening. In addition to that, God revealed further that he is coming to propose to her and that is her future husband. She was able to receive light and direction in the place of prayer. The Holy Spirit praying through you when you pray in tongues keeps all things sorted, to the minutest of details. In the same way that we speak secrets unto God when we pray in tongues, God reveals secrets to us when we pray in tongues.

Praying in tongues keeps your life deeply rooted in grace. In the same way that an anchor steadies a ship, praying in tongues enhances your life and keeps you from being tossed to and fro with every passing wind. It aligns you with the perfect will of God for your life. Yes, we are made to understand that the Spirit intercedes [before God] on behalf of God's people in accordance with God's will.

"In the same way the Spirit [comes to us and] helps us in our weakness. We do not know what prayer to offer or how to offer it as we should, but the Spirit Himself [knows our need and at the right time] intercedes on our behalf with sighs and groanings

too deep for words." Romans 8:26.

- **Generates inner strength**

Praying in tongues helps you to generate strength in the place of prayer. The Holy Spirit assists you in overcoming your weakness and makes prayer pleasurable. He gives strength in that place where we are feeble and struggling to generate power to pray. We are 'weak' in the place of prayer in that we do not have the human capacity to pray as often and as much as we ought to. However, when we pray in tongues, we are girded with strength to recognize we need to pray. Not only that, we are infused with the strength we need to achieve this.

In terms of consistency, and also in terms of volume the Holy Spirit energizes us. Apart from strengthening our capacity to pray as we ought, through praying in tongues, we are empowered to pray and get sustained in the place of prayer. By praying in tongues, we are fuelled to pray for longer.

"Meanwhile, the moment we get tired in the waiting, God's Spirit is right alongside helping us along. If we don't know how or what to pray, it doesn't matter. He does our praying in and for us, making prayer out of our wordless sighs, our

55

aching groans. He knows us far better than we know ourselves, knows or pregnant condition, and keeps us present before God. That's why we can be so sure that every detail in our lives of love for God is worked into something good."

Rom. 8:26-28. The Message.

- It enhances having a life dedicated to detailed and consistent prayer

Another benefit of praying in tongues is that you get to address every aspect of your life without leaving a single one out. Many times, we are at a loss on what exactly we need to pray about. However, when we switch into praying in tongues over a particular situation, the Holy Spirit dwells on every aspect of what we are praying for without leaving out the vitals.

We do not know what to pray for. We do not know how to go into depths of those things we need to pray for. At this point, we can switch to the tongues and pray until we get a release in our hearts. The Holy Spirit will search out every aspect and touch every single issue. No grain will be left untouched. The smallest detail will receive attention and God will be glorified. The Holy Spirit praying through us when we pray in tongues keeps us in tune with God.

Because the Holy Spirit helps us when we pray, He addresses the details of every situation without skipping any aspect. When we pray in understanding and engage our intellect, there is a probability to skip the details. For instance, if you put your prayer list before you and take each after the other, you can pray in understanding first and then move on to pray in tongues. Praying in understanding enables your mind to know the direction of the prayer. Praying in tongues then create volume and depth around each prayer as you roll things over to God while praying in tongues. Romans 8:26.

- **Praying in tongues gives you deep spiritual insight**

Praying in tongues ushers you into a deeper level of understanding of the scriptures. The bible says holy men wrote the scriptures as they were inspired by the Holy Spirit. In other words, these holy men spoke as they were moved by the Holy Ghost. 2 Peter 1:21.

Praying in tongues opens up the channels of your spirit to receive unusual understanding of the thoughts and intents of God. Not only that; praying in tongues gives you revelation and deep spiritual insight to fathom the depth of the riches of the wisdom and knowledge of God. As an offshoot, your words carry great weight because you also become infused with the unusual wisdom of God to interpret enigma.

Praying in tongues joins your spirit to the Spirit of God in the place of intimate and intense prayers; you begin to open up portals (step into dimensions of mysteries) through praying in tongues. You thus access realms that are beyond your human intellectual capacity. You operate with a unique knowledge of witty inventions.

"Oh, the depth of the riches of the wisdom and knowledge of God! How unsearchable his judgments, and his paths beyond tracing out."
Romans 11:33.

- **Praying in tongues fortifies your prayer life.**

Aside being a means of communication with God, prayer is actual warfare in the spirit. Praying in tongues loads up your arsenal and better equips you to engage the enemy in warfare. It confuses the enemy because he cannot know your move. Since you are not praying in understanding, praying in tongues adds a dimension of mystery to your prayers.

While sending out the disciples, they were charged to

preach the gospel to every creature. In arming them to combat every opposition that the devil may throw on their paths, the bible talks about 'signs' that shall follow those who believe. The first one on the list is that they will cast out devils in the name of Jesus. This is followed being endowed with the ability to speak in tongues. It goes further to say they shall take serpents and it shall not hurt them. This is sign to us that being able to speak in tongues is actually a weapon against the devil; our adversary who prowls and looks for who to devour. Mark 16:15-18.

- **Praying in tongues gives you boldness to witness**

Praying in tongues prepares you for evangelistic work. The bible says we have received the ministry of reconciliation. We are ambassadors of the kingdom of God. When we pray in tongues, our words carry grace to minister to a lost soul. The bible assures that we will receive power after the Holy Ghost is come upon us. After receiving that enablement of the Spirit, we will then become witnesses from our immediate environment and spread to the farthest part of the earth.

"... ye shall receive power, after that the Holy Ghost

is come upon you: and ye shall be witnesses unto me both in Jerusalem, and in all Judaea, and in Samaria, and unto the uttermost part of the earth." Acts 1:8.

How to be Filled with the Holy Spirit

4

How to be Filled with the Holy Spirit

WE HAVE THIS treasure in earthen vessels; so says the bible in 2 Corinthians 4:7. In other words, as believers, we carry the essence of God in our earthly body of clay. The Holy Spirit of God can turn our recreated human spirits into His abode and operate from within us. That means as humans; flesh and blood, we can become God's earthly administrative office with the headquarters located in the heavens. We can have a dynamic operation of the celestial in our mortal bodies.

As God's children, heaven responds when we call upon the name of the Lord. And this is the confidence that we have in Him. We have the assurance that if we ask anything according to God's will; the hosts of heaven stand at attention to deliver it to us.

Having been assured of being endowed with the Holy Spirit, every child of God is expected to come boldly to the throne of grace to receive this gift. After being filled, the Spirit of God springs up in us and becomes a mighty river that waters the world around us.

Becoming acquainted with the person of the Holy Ghost is not enough, the real joy is to own it. That is the focus of this chapter. In Acts 2, the disciples waited eagerly for it. Their hearts burned within them as they patiently wait to be endued with power from on high. In no time, every one of them in that room received the Holy Spirit. For all who wait patiently for the promise of the Father, the assurance of receiving it still stands.

Becoming God's child by accepting the offer of salvation and accepting Jesus as your Lord and Saviour subscribes you to His family. When you do that, you cross over from death unto life. In that instant, you become a citizen of heaven. In addition to that privilege, you become an heir of God, and a joint-heir with Christ. Realizing these spiritual truths deepens your confidence. From that point, you can enjoy the unlimited riches of God hidden in Christ. Becoming born again opens portals unto you. It unlocks realms that were hitherto slammed against you.

When you receive Jesus, your spirit is quickened. That is, your spirit comes alive and can easily connect to the Spirit of God. At this point, you must not embrace the fear of inadequacy in any form. The 'whatsoever' promises in the word of God is for the 'whosoever'. Now, you can lay hold of great promises in the scriptures because you belong to God. You are God's own and always call to heart that having been received into the family of God; you can shout 'Abba Father'. Call to heart that in the Aramaic language, 'Abba' is a child's fond way of saying 'father'. In contemporary times, it is the same as a child wrapping his/her tiny arms around the father and saying 'daddy'.

Also, by saying 'Abba'; you can call upon God in the most intimate way. You can reach out to Him in reverence, in adoration or in the simplest form of lovingly gazing into the eyes of a Father who has decided to love you with an everlasting love. Calling on God as 'Father' is a statement acknowledging your Source. It is an affirmation of the Rock from which you were hewn, the quarry from which you were dug. Beyond being a term for affection, 'Abba' is also a form of reverencing the awesomeness of God. It is the language of acknowledging the One whose life breathes life into every fiber of your being and sustains you.

How do I receive the gift of the Holy Spirit?

Acknowledge that God is willing to give you

At the core of His being, God is a giver. Fundamentally, we are made to realize that He gave His only begotten Son to us because He loves us. John 3:16. God is a 'fiery' lover who loves extravagantly and gives passionately without holding back.

The first step to receiving the Holy Spirit is to acknowledge the fact that God is willing and ready to endow you with the Holy Spirit. He owns every good and perfect gift and gives all who asks Him liberally.

"Every good gift and every perfect gift is from above, and cometh down from the Father of lights, with whom is no variableness, neither shadow of turning." James 1:17.

While shedding light on James 1:17, The Message Translation of this passage says that the gifts that God gives are rivers of light cascading down from the Father of Light with whom there is nothing deceitful.

If God promised a gift, He will sure give it to you. He owns every good and perfect gift. Not only that, He is willing to give you such gifts.

The Holy Spirit is a good gift. God is willing to bless you with that wonderful gift so that your life can take a new dimension in being impactful and meaningful. Be rest assured that when you go to God, He will freely bless you with the gift of His Spirit.

There is also another bible verse that inspires us to acknowledge that God is willing to give the Holy Ghost to all who desire and ask for it. The bible acknowledges that no father will give his child a scorpion if the child asks for an egg. In the same vein, when a child asks for bread, no earthly father will give such a child a scorpion. As earthly fathers are kind towards their children being nurtured with love and affection, God in His sovereignty will not neglect those who ask for the gift of the Holy Spirit.

11"If a son shall ask bread of any of you that is a father, will he give him a stone? Or if he ask a fish, will he for a fish give him a serpent?
12 Or if shall ask an egg, will he offer him a scorpion?
13 If ye then, being evil, know how to give good gifts

unto your children: how much more shall your heavenly Father give the Holy Spirit to them that ask him?" Luke 11:11-13.

Open your heart and be expectant

In the book of Acts, precisely the third chapter; we read an account of a lame man who received his healing as Peter and John were going up to the temple at the time of prayer. The man has been crippled all his life and everyday they brought him to the gate called 'beautiful' in order to ask alms from those going inside the temple.

His story changed when he met Peter and John. When they told him to look at them, the bible records that the man 'gave them his attention". Acts 3:4. His gaze was totally fixed on these two men. He was full of expectation to receive what they had to offer. The Living Bible translation says *'the lame man looked at them eagerly, expecting a gift'.* He was ready to take and possess everything in their custody that was meant for his life to improve. Expectation births miracles. Because his expectation was top notch, he got his healing.

Another individual who got a miracle from having a

strong expectation is the woman with the issue of blood. Prior to meeting Jesus, she kept her self talk direct. She says to herself every time, *'if I can only touch His garments, I shall be made whole'*. Mark 5:26-33. Before she actually met Jesus and pressed through the crowd, the woman with the issue of blood rehearsed her moves and clearly defined her mission.

You must constantly expect the in-filling of the Holy Spirit. Having an expectation opens your heart to receive. Forget every misconception you have had so far. With the faith of a child, let your heart open up and expect God for a visitation. As you worship in the comfort of your home, as you enjoy a warm shower, the baptism of the Holy Spirit can occur. It does not necessarily have to happen when you are reading the bible or when you are in church. God sees your heart and He will definitely honour your faith.

Create an atmosphere for miracles around you

At the beginning of creation in Genesis 1:1, the Holy Spirit was hovering over the darkness that was prevalent at that point. He was present. In your day to day living, make room for the Spirit of God to be actively engaged in everything you do. Let the Spirit of God find an atmosphere of expression where you are. Soak up the scriptures and meditate in your heart. Immerse your surroundings with worship songs that refresh your spirit.

At all points, invite God in everything you are involved in. As you drive to work, commune with Him. As you lay on the bed, talk to Him. You will be so amazed at how easy it will be for the Holy Spirit to be drawn to you. The Holy Spirit is actually a person and has feelings. Let the Holy Spirit know that you crave having an intimate fellowship with Him.

Request for hands to be laid on you

One of the ways to receive spiritual gifts is through the laying on of hands. The bible is filled with many instances narrating such occurrence. According to Deuteronomy 34:9, Joshua the son of Nun was filled with the spirit of wisdom because Moses laid hands on him. The believers in Samaria received the Holy Spirit because Peter and John placed their hands on them. Acts 8:16-17. After having an encounter with Jesus, Saul (who later became Paul) became blind. Ananias went to him as instructed by God and laid his hands on him. Two things happened instantly. First of all, Saul regained his sight. In addition, he was filled with the Holy Spirit. After that he got baptized. Acts 9:17-18.

Later on, when Paul (formerly Saul) arrived at Ephesus, he found some disciples and talked to them about the Holy Spirit. After expounding the scriptures to them, he placed his hands on them and they received the Holy Spirit and spoke in tongues. Like these people in Ephesus, you can ask those who are already filled with the Holy Spirit to lay their hands on you in order to receive the in-filling of the Holy Spirit with the vocal evidence of speaking in tongues.

Just ask for it

God is a good God. Let that truth sink into your spirit. He loves you tenderly and cares for you affectionately. There are different places where the word of God invites you to make your request known unto God. You are expected to show up at the throne of grace. And God expects you to show up with courage. You are only expected to ask so that you can receive. You must knock in order for the door to be opened, and you only need to seek in order for you to find. Mathew 7:7.

Go to God with a child-like faith. Knock the door. Ask for the gift of the Holy Spirit and trust God to make good His words in your life. He is trustworthy!

Here are few words that can serve as guide in calling on God to endow you with the gift of the Holy Spirit.

Dear Lord,
I acknowledge You as the source of every good thing. Thanks for the gift of the Holy Spirit. Thanks for the assurance I have in your word. Lord, I open up my heart to receive this gift. I pray Lord that you fill me up with your Holy Spirit with the evidence of speaking in tongues. I receive this gift with thanksgiving. For I pray in the name of Jesus.

The Promise
is unto You

5

The Promise is unto You

WHAT IS THE most precious gift you have ever received? All of us love gifts. We look forward to being surprised with thoughtful gifts from time to time. It hits differently when the gift came from someone who loves you deeply, and who you love in the same fashion. Gifts communicate to us. They touch our souls and reminds us of how loved we are and how we are thought of as valuable. That explains why precious gifts are treasured.

Having received the Holy Spirit, you need to understand how to ensure His presence in your life thrives so that you can constantly enjoy the numerous benefits that are attached to being in possession of this amazing gift. Until you realize how precious the Holy Spirit is and the difference His presence makes in your life, you might be unable to guard it jealously.

According to the rendition of the New Century Version of Ephesians 4:30; the Holy Spirit is God's proof that you belong to Him. In other words, it is God's seal of ownership placed on you. David realized the importance of being constantly filled with the Spirit of the living God. When he fell into sin, he prayed unto God *'do not take your Holy Spirit away from me'.* Psalms 51:11.

David knew that to be without the Holy Spirit is to be spiritually dead. Life without the Holy Spirit reckons with being void, spiritually empty and powerless. The Holy Spirit indwelling a child of God is what brings about the touch of the supernatural that makes life worth living.

Grieve not the Holy Spirit

The Holy Spirit can be driven away. His operations in our lives can be stifled. We can hinder His moves and paralyze His deeds through the way we relate with Him in our day to day living. A deeper study of Ephesians 4:30-32 from more bible translations will shed light on this deep truth.

"... the Holy Spirit has sealed you in Jesus Christ... never grieve the Spirit of God or take for granted

his holy influence in your life."
(The Passion Translation).

"... do not grieve the Holy Spirit of God [but seek to please Him], by whom you were sealed and marked [branded as God's own]... (The Amplified).

"... don't make the Holy Spirit sad. God gave you His Spirit as proof that you belong to Him..."

Our ways of living can grieve the Holy Spirit. How do you conduct your life? As a Christian, after receiving the Holy Spirit, your tongue becomes a spring of life. To that end, it can no longer worship God and curse simultaneously. Fresh water and salt water cannot flow from the same spring. A fig tree cannot bear olives, in the same way that a grapevine cannot bear figs.

Having the Holy Spirit operating through our lives calls us to higher living. His presence behoves us to holy living. It calls us to rise higher and attain to righteous living. We are expected to walk worthy of the Lord. In God's Word Translation of Ephesians 4:30, we are admonished; *'don't give God's Holy Spirit any reason to be upset with you ...'* As God's children, we are instructed on how to go about this.

31 "Get rid of your bitterness, hot tempers, anger, loud quarreling, cursing, and hatred.
32 Be kind to each other, sympathetic, forgiving each other as God has forgiven you through Christ."

The function of the Holy Spirit resident in you goes beyond speaking in tongues. Having been taken over by the Spirit of God, your mode of living must witness a shift because of how God's presence is now expressed through you. The aura of the supernatural around you must ooze out effortlessly.

Vessels unto honour

As God's children, we are vessels unto honour. As we purify our hearts and our hands, we are made fit to serve our King's purpose. The man that is cleansed will be an instrument for noble purposes. Such a holy vessel will be an instrument reserved for assignments of higher calling, useful to the Master and prepared to do every good work. 2 Timothy 2:20-22.

Beyond praying in tongues, there are specific assignments that God have ordained for you before you were brought forth from eternity into time.

Owning the Spirit of God as yours and being conscious of the in-dwelling of this gift enables you to thrive in your God-ordained assignment.

Within your local assembly, or largely within the body of Christ, there is a place where your feet have been planted and God expects you to occupy so that you can be His mouthpiece. The Holy Spirit operating within you enables you to know how to function as a vessel unto a higher calling.

You must build a strong relationship with the Holy Spirit to know the heart of God for every situation. Being alert in the spirit will quicken you to pick the promptings of the Holy Spirit and know what is required of you every step of the way.

There is no way you can occupy your sphere of influence in God's kingdom without being full of the Holy Spirit. As you take time to pray, you will hear expressly from God and directed on how to go about it. There are examples in the bible.

In the church in Antioch, there were certain people who came together to fast and pray. The presence of the Holy Spirit was strong amongst them. As they were communing with the Lord in that gathering, the

Holy Spirit asked that Barnabas and Saul should be separated for a special work that God has prepared for them. These disciples fasted and prayed some more, laid hands on the appointed people and sent them out to accomplish the task that God apportioned for them.

The task of the Holy Spirit is beyond your private life. In the bigger circle, at the global scene, as far as the gospel of the Lord Jesus is concerned; God has reserved a place for you. Being aware of this truth will encourage you to take your relationship with the Holy Spirit serious. As believers, we have been assigned with the ministry of reconciliation. We have been assigned to reach out to the world with the gospel of the Lord Jesus Christ. The Spirit of God will play a role in our lives regarding the 'ministry' that God has apportioned for us.

Many Christians will be called into the ministry in different capacities. In this instance, there will be those called to be music ministers, the Holy Spirit will anoint their lyrics to bring healing to people all over the world. There are other Christians whose ministry it is to reach out to those in the hospital. Others will be sent to the prison as their mission field. There will be those who will be called into the pulpit ministry. Recognizing how vital the help of the Holy Spirit is to whatever ministry you have been called to will trigger your desire to take His presence in your life as a rare privilege, one that must be treated with utmost honour.

As a parent, you can be called to raise an outstanding child to represent the interest of God for a particular generation. As a Christian business person, you can be equipped to be a kingdom financier. The promise of the Holy Spirit is unto you. His presence is for you to own. You need Him. He must walk with you and hold your hands as you walk the path marked out for you as a child of God, and as someone who has been appointed to be partner with the Holy Spirit in representing the interest of the kingdom of God.

The Holy Spirit helps you as an individual. He also helps you in the ministry assigned to the unbelieving people outside the church. It does not end there. The Holy Spirit is intended to also strengthen those within a church through you.

The edification of the church

Iron sharpens iron. As Christians, we are encouraged

to consider how to spur one another on in our faith. To that end, we are warned against standing alone. As tiny sparks come together, they create a big fire that is not easily put out. We must not neglect our church meetings; rather we must encourage and warm each other.

When we come together during our fellowship meetings, each person must come with something spiritually edifying for everyone. One person has a psalm, another has a teaching, and another has a revelation or a tongue with interpretation.

As the body of Christ, the Holy Spirit inside each of us makes our meetings life-giving. To that end, when you receive the Holy Spirit, there is a deposit of edification intended for the church of God to grow by put inside of you. Receiving the Holy Spirit does not end at the point of being able to speak in tongues and enjoy the benefits. The grace the Holy Spirit brings extends to the local assembly (church/fellowship) where you meet with the other believers regularly.

Always remember that there are sparks in each of God's children. When we all come together, we generate a spiritual inferno that can create warmth for us and wreck havoc in the kingdom of darkness. One of the reasons you must own the gift of God resident on the inside of you is to retain your vitality in the larger family of God where you belong.

The Holy Spirit edifies us, gives us direction and infuses spiritual vigour in our Christian walk. He is the fullness of God. He fills all things. He opens the scriptures unto us. Restricting the Holy Spirit to speaking in tongues alone is like restricting our mobile telephones to receiving phone calls alone. There are other vital functions that our devices can perform. We must strive to harness the full potential of the gift of God unto us.

The revealer of all things

The promise of the Father is unto you! The Holy Spirit of God is an awesome companion. He reveals the deep things. He is the revealer of truth. The hidden things belong unto our God. The things that are revealed unto us are for us and for our children. Deuteronomy 29:29.

There are secret things. The Holy Spirit gives the unveiling unto us as we unite with Him and yield ourselves in consecration to the higher calling unto which God has appointed us.

The men of old who walked with God in an intimate fashion operated under the influence of the Spirit of the living God. When Gehazi ran after Naaman to collect gifts from him, in the physical realm, Gehazi did not inform Elisha. When he returned with the gifts and his master asked him where he had been. He lied and told him *'your servant went nowhere'.* In telling him his offence, Elisha stated *'my spirit went with you'.* 2 Kings 5:25-27.

As a man of God full of the Spirit of God, he knew what was taking place without leaving the same location. The Spirit of God revealed the sins of Gehazi. The Spirit of God reveals the deep things. It captures what is concealed and lay it bare to the person walking by the guidance of the Holy Spirit.

On another occasion, the king of Aram felt one of his servants was a spy (2 Kings 6:11). His officers assured him none of them was. Going further, they stated, 'Elisha, the prophet who is in Israel tells the king of Israel the very words he speaks in his bedroom'. In other words, Elisha could hear the words that the king spoke with his officers right inside his palace. As those words were dropping from the king's mouth, God's Spirit was revealing everything to Prophet Elisha. The Holy Spirit reveals deep things.

In the book of Acts, Ananias and Sapphira sold a piece of land and brought the money to the church. They connived and lied about the actual amount the land was sold for. While rebuking them, Peter asked them *'why has Satan filled your heart and made you lie to the Holy Spirit'*? Acts 5:1-11.

The Spirit of God reveals what crouches in the hearts of men and women. You cannot run the Christian race successfully without embracing the fullness of the operations of the Holy Spirit. His operations cut across all the different facets of your life.

Made in United States
North Haven, CT
15 August 2024